World Heritage Minescape : Looking South-East to the Great Wall of Dadbe (and lagoon where the croco

he German tourist). With Ranger Mine in the foreground and Djabilukku (Jabiluka) further to the North.

jabiluka

jabiluka honey

NEW & SELECTED POEMS

RICHARD HILLMAN

RICHARD HILLMAN

was born in 1964. He grew up in the outer western suburbs of Sydney. In 1994 he moved to Adelaide with wife Allison ("the concrete goddess who gathers no moss") and their three children Lachlan, Shanyn and Bronte. His career as a writer has included radio talkback shows, live internet performances, and readings at many of Australia's most well known literary establishments. His poetry has been published widely throughout Australia, New Zealand, Europe, and the USA. He has volunteered much of his spare time to editing various magazines, journals and anthologies, including SideWaLK: *an antipodean journal of poetics and poetry.*

BY THE SAME AUTHOR

poetry
mending the dingo fence
gone up river
no grounds

anthologies
flow: friendly street reader #25
(with Heather Sladdin)

jabiluka honey

NEW & SELECTED POEMS

RICHARD HILLMAN

PHOTOGRAPHY

JEFF DALE

BOOKENDS BOOKS

2003

First published 2003 by Bookends Books, 136 Unley Road, Unley SA 5061

Rob Scott   bookends.bookshop@adelaide.on.net

National Library of Australia
Cataloguing-in-Publication entry
Hillman, Richard, 1964-.
    Jabiluka Honey
ISBN   1 876725 30 3
    1. Australian poetry — 20th century. I. Title. II. Author.
    2. Australian poetry — Environment. I. Title. II. Author.
A821.3

Cover art: *"Dying River, Far North"* Tim John, 1983;
Original artwork supplied courtesy of Glen Murdoch -
photography courtesy of Duncan Kentish Fine Art, Adelaide.

Design/layout /typography by Jeff Dale, *PageCurl Graphics*, Crafers SA.
Frontispiece: *Kakadu:World Heritage Minescape*, Jeff Dale, 1986.
Illustrative photography by Jeff Dale.   jed49@ozemail.com.au

Printed and bound in Australia by CM Digital, Adelaide, 2003.

For Allison Mary Hillman

the concrete goddess who
gathers no moss

FOREWORD

To act purely seems not to be desired; people want something else –
a position that is already compromised. There are only trite things
that can be said. It comes as a shock to discover that the poet is not
the person you know.

I discovered that I had set myself a special task: to write the text I
was writing backwards. In other words, the first sentence comes
last, the second last sentence second last. The text generates itself
by being written backwards.

The notion of an Australian landscape is rather overestimated. It's
like those explorers off in search of somewhere and coming back
empty-handed, if at all. Oh yes, we had to kill the horses to use the
hides to make a boat in order to cross the river, then when we got to
the other side we found we couldn't proceed and the horses dead.
We might have ferried pointlessly backwards and forwards across
the stream for days. After all, it wasn't very big. But the crocodiles
had got the smell of us – and that was that.

Others go by car, looking.

When you come back to wherever you come back to you can do
various things – like dump objects here and there as a sort of
revenge against future archaeologists. My house in Braddon ended
up with mudshells from the mangroves near Aurukun and oyster
shells from Orchid Point. Maybe. I forget. There were round
boulders from the Murrumbidgee too. It's hard to divest the mind.
It divests itself in other ways and creates other archaeologies.

The best poetry sets out not to be poetry – certainly not to be poetic, though we acquire little habits here and there, moves we have to rid ourselves of. The task here is to undo the nation by inventing it – by a ruthless abandoning of all previous forms and mannerisms which do nothing more than trumpet our triumph into a very near oblivion. It is why the explorers may never be an obsolete thing, and year by year we discover the trees where they carved their names were truly enduring things, even if they appear modest even now and haven't aged a day since whenever then was. I'm thinking of Landsborough on the Georgina.

The father is always absent - for it is a landscape in which ancestry fades, or is lost in that instant forgetting by street sign which passes for urban memorialisation. In looking the child creates its own ancestry – which becomes by default the ancestry of the watching parent. The parent is the child of the child – for the child seems to be in possession of a history the parent never had or somehow mislaid.

Unless you take a 'snap' there is a very real risk that it never existed.

Dr. John von Sturmer
Thursday, 30 January 2003

CONTENTS

The Barrage

I gaze across the atmospheric gap
of your two hundred year dream
& find green lobsters turning childhood-blue
in salt-water footprints beneath
the dredge-swollen mouth.

With tentacles they snorkel
for sacred sites
like surface weeds
on candidly low Coorong tides,
a culture of inquiry staining
their tenacious tips
with barrages of thought.

They rub wounds
with salt-skinned words,
then beach
like judges on a sand bar
not knowing whether the tide's in
or out, waiting perhaps
for Murray's ground water sunset
to release them.

Jabiluka Honey

My rusty HQ Holden rainbows out
        a chemical canoe
floating on the floodplain's fluid surface.

Sweating miles of straight goanna-backed road
        I dream I am
an alligator on an alien landscape
        fish-tailing through warm serum currents
in a womb of filtered light-trees.

Inspecting an unexpected silence
        I feel as if I'm approaching
something I've never left.

All around me
        the yellow hair of a lover
tiny insect legs
        caught in the sticky honey of a golden twilight

& emptiness.

Beyond her soft amber strands

I see a cancer upon her moist face
as an unknown fibre falls
    & casts a shadow
upon my own.

In the shaven-headed distance
    tabletop stumps open palms
leave silver coins in afternoon sun.

Tarnished roots
    fingerprint
the clinging earth.

From open cut mine
    dry dust irritates
the wide dirt ruts of restless eyes
    & sun-broken skin
when I raise a reckless hand
    to brush ground brown hair
from my face.

Beneath tender treeline
    I gather stock
on the steamy edge of a swamp
    & release a sigh of belief.

At day's end
         there's a canvas tent
& filtered water from Uranium Falls.

A near comatose algae
         touches everything
I haven't touched.

Covers fluid trails
         green mangrove scars
& salt-laced sand stains.

An endless shoreline stubble
         corrugated as soap
squeezed through a sponge

& these starless strands of hair.

Gone Up River

1. Twilight

I don't know where I am, stretched out
& staring into lighter-fluid sky from the
backseat of my scratched midnight blue HQ
Holden with Snake Catchers bumper sticker stuck
to its cleanly slashed cream-vinyl upholstery
telling myself, This is not a dream —

My father has gone up river
& I have to find him

Yet he is a tidal vision
floating backwards & forwards
like the Murray

I don't know . . . at what point
do I enter

When I step onto the sand
-raw bank people stare
as if they recognise me

But they're not looking at me

They see themselves in my eyes
collecting the naked bodies of trees
washed downstream on wasting tide

The Evening Star has camped in colour
on the pale rim of my windshield, a still
photograph of Pegasus launching, perhaps
from Cape Canaveral, into the sun

6

2. Searching

I follow his wet/dry trail
& in every newly met town
deal with variations on a theme —

I stop for petrol & water
& a shadow places a flier beneath
the remaining window wiper
while my back is turned in payment

It reads:
A Musical For The Family —
DON'T KNOCK NOAH!
as if my car isn't an ark
        & every animal I pass
        hasn't been flattened
        beneath the wheels of civilization

in THE REVIVAL TENT
Admission FREE!
— as if I need permission
to enter

I take this road
but the sign I've just passed says
STOP! REVIVE! SURVIVE!

                like a conspiracy

The mobile feast has left its marks
on the side of the road
discarded fliers float
out of reach & beyond
I see the river's edge

3. The River

I trace the river's outline
with wheels like hands
I don't wish to dirty

I stare through glass
& dark mud clings to my eyes
from trees which hang
their heads in shame
as I pass

I drive up river
beneath the stooping black
accusations of trees
but there's no going back no
place to turn away

4. Camping With Revivalists

In night's tent
I breathe the pure oxygen of longing
& its imported fumes: Tea Tree Oil
in steaming water

I feel as if I'm a watery-flat expanse
waiting to be walked upon by
cultural missionaries searching
for a mythical shoreline, cosmic leap
into the dustbowl of togetherness
& I wonder, why they expect this to be
sufficient absolution from what it is
to be human

The river murmurs
words which I cannot make out
& on its moon-creased surface
white skeletons float

In exile

5. Living Riverscape

I've woken
from a fog of dreams
in the artists' camp
beside the river
& I can almost see
through the canvas

Beyond the tent flap
dawn's warm hand
spreads slow fingers

Outside, I cup water
to lips, nourish the pulse
inside my head

The river wind plays
on my naked skin, &
I almost feel alive

among the apprehensive dead —

dry   stump   damp   sand

Fallen trees collect at my feet
like the cold armour of angels

6.   Lost

Somewhere
day has become a shallow pathway
round broken iron-bark
                        & red-eyed brolga
who count
the wry steps of humanity
from split-timber sanctuaries

Sometimes
I glimpse the river
through the opening eyelashes
of sleepless trees

It is late
I drive on tinder
trying not to set the river on fire

7. Snake Trail

River snakes into view
& I hear laughter curling
water round a snag

Sensing my father
             somewhere near
I take a look around

In still frame
a snared Yellow-Bellied Black Snake
lies upon the bank
head absorbed in heat
listening out for my approach, or
waiting for me to pass —
                            there is doubt
in the fall of a seed, an ambiguous arrival
in the snap of a twig, a footfall
that is neither friend nor foe

I tread slowly
towards my distant relative's
cold   dead   eyes

8. Blood Trail

I follow blood lines
& trees watch / shadow
each staggered step

Stained leaves tremble
& branches flinch
on contact whilst
shadows play dappled
shapes upon my face

A snake serrates
my vision trail

Bone white teeth
intersect skin
darkness
bleeds from my lips

I am close now
I can smell him
on my bark-rough skin
as if I've touched

                    the very rawness
                    of his intentions

There is blood
on my splintered hands
& the sun has turned
a deep red against
the swollen grain
of my exposed flesh

9. The Clearing

Skins hang from loose
lengths of wood inserted
between back to back trees

Around a fire voices
in discontinuous narrative
fix a price so low it appears
to bear no relation
to what has been done

Faces turn towards mine
& I sense the horror
in my burning eyes
bending back as a tree
to face what lies beyond
myself

10. Tree & Water

In shallows beyond the clearing
my father's hands have turned
to light & sun-steamed foliage
grasps at last rays of happiness

The sweat of my green sense sucks
words from hostile soil

Roots build bridges
between sky & water
& branches reach for a visual Babel
as ideas run as sap
through timber veins
& a flat red river
turns tinder-sour thoughts
into something
ordinary

11. The Eleventh Hour

I sleep on loamy bank
& wake beneath stars

I see shadows among trees
which are not shadows
but death's gift of shapes

The world continues
revolving round the sun
& moon & stars & clouds
& day & night & day
flows on, the patterns
changing little
by little

I feel sun
toiling on green skin

Resting elsewhere the sun leaves
rain to wipe its fingerprints
from river's mirror surface

Then the floods, the young

trees drowning & the old
holding fast the stiff bodies
of struggling saplings
in outstretched arms before
the sagging sun drinks
with skin-cracked lips
from leaf & spine

I stand tall upon the bank
until I feel the axe's salted
-blade against my wooden legs

I fall into a silence
that does not cry out
nor warn, only the world
turning sideways as I roll
on the returning river's
wake of water

I toss & turn
on sheets of stolen dreams

float downstream
on the ebb-tide's falling
level of attraction
as a vision drifting towards
the pillow of a new land

Familiar hands
lift my naked body
from this water bed
& carry me
to higher ground

When I open my eyes
I can see my old Holden
scratched & rusted
on the farthest shore

Retribution

The dusty land's neither good, nor bad
and the river runs when it's wet —
the barren earth's not a metaphor
and the muddy water's beyond morality
but we live in doubt with drought
or drown in unexpected downpour
cursing seasons, or fired up about a frost
the inclement temperament
and its vernacular companion surround
Nature, as if expectant country voices
were ring-barking trees or culling roos, and
salt-sucked skies bring no relief from
hot air on parched lips, the funnel-web
nights inject their venom
into your sleeping form, disturb your dreams
until there is nothing but sagging skin
over old bones and, a feeling
that there is no one left to blame
but yourself.

Totem I

On the kookaburra's kitchen table
there's a borrowed recipe book,
without a plot. She turns the cover back
like a garden rock, & a lizard (a small,
grey-yellow gecko with padded feet
& bulging round eyes) barks across
the ant-mapped surface of her dream,
perhaps returning to its own like an echo.
The kookaburra chuckles with a hunter's
hunger — tuckatuckatuckatuckatuckatuckal
tuckaltuckaltuckatucka — while the gecko
searches for the source of that sound
as if he'd heard his mother calling,
the bush tucker bird swoops down, grins
as she gobbles up what she has found.

Totem II

I offer you my lizard lips,
my reptile tongue.
I peel back my scales
& expose my breast.
But you just laugh
like a kookaburra,
swoop down upon me
leave
my blood upon the ground,
your belly full.

Beyond Eucla

I'm running in dust, drought bitten
feet over roads beyond rural time
searching for a rest, the Nullarbor
a truck stop 300 ks out of Eucla
an unfamiliar face, a mozzie net
sand flies in my eyes & the price
of water, bore or plastic bottled
the stringent smell of petrol fumes
a motel room where the vacancy sign
doesn't work
where the cook picks his nose
& the heat doesn't care
whether you win or lose

Dead Wood

viewing a canoe tree at the
Murray-Darling Rivers junction

I never wanted to draw
this picture of lifelessness
through your eyes,
but you are seeing me
with arms around this gutted tree
as if she were my mother.

the fish has lost its smell
hanging on Boydian wire

Reeds carry spears like mourners
but there is no dancing.

Roots hang grey & shrivelled
like severed birth cords.

The cut shape of a canoe
rounded like a word
or the hollow of a woman
who has paused to give birth
on the edge of falling.

Any moment now
she will break away,
swim downstream
& look for her children.

ancient canoe tree. old woman. you tell me things. your
belly hollow. looking at me. wallowing in green muddy
muck. leaning down to drink. surrounded by spears.
memories. sturt's camp in reeds. not far from where you
lean. on your sorrow. old canoe woman you don't swim.
your head bent in sadness. mourning. for children lost in
water. old fella murray he just gobbled them up like little
fish. old mother. you've been fishing for your children a
long time. but they have not come back. perhaps that fella
from the mining company. he come fishing for those
children too.

Locust Plague At Terowie

We pull into Terowie's two-pump service station
the kids still in pjs
& the dry ground covered
in lost locusts

insects
as large as hitch-hikers
get inside our car
& in our hair
& the kids run bare-foot
across their backs
with tiny wings sticking up
between their toes

& the woman at the counter
complains about the heat
that hasn't arrived
yet doesn't want the kids
to open the soft drink fridge
unless they know what they want

& by the time I pay for the gas
the bugs are inside the grill

& inside the vents

clutching the windshield wipers

as if they've decided to come along for the ride

& I don't blame them

for their sudden sense of direction

for wanting

to get away from the place.

Dance Of The Willy-Willys

The sun has begun to suck
upon the surface of our senses
& Shanyn wants me to stop the car
& take photographs of willy-willys
in the heat's fifty degree opera:

muddy sun-spun ballerinas
above dusty dry ground
drag red earth partners skyward
auditioning on a rough stage
where smoke twists away
from dirty factory chimneys
& sprawl into suburban distances
constructions that only exist out here
in mind's hell.

When we drive on, Shanyn reflects:
if there were brickworks in heaven
all the clouds would be castles —

but it's too damn hot to argue
&, to keep the peace
I've taken a wide angled picture
for her bedroom wall.

Ghosts Of Nyngan Hunger

The dead are still with us
lining the sides of the road
like a guard of honour
for passing ghosts.

Perhaps we are already dead.
The blur we see outside our window
simply a reflection of what we once were, or are;
another life we haven't caught up with
or, trapped in the process of catching up,
we continue to drive, moving ourselves
beyond range, leaving these things
out of reach.

It's as if by staying mobile
our wish to reach out to them
might remain constant.

It's as if such gestures
were apparitions, mirages
on the tip of a road reflecting
our desire to reach ourselves,
our own ghosts.

Everything on this landscape
is yelling at me to drive faster;
to escape the constancy,
the ordinariness,
the repetition of farmland:
the slow turning of giant sprinklers,
the rugged ruts in ploughed fields,
the circularity of silos.

The colours of sky & earth
scream at me
& smells lift as sweat
from every sun-touched acre
(refusing me excluding me repulsing me)
& the kids can't get their windows up
quick enough,
telling me to drive faster,
to get away from the rural pong
& filth & stench

& I feel the force,
the pressure to move beyond
these mounds of rolled wheat, beyond
these clusters of rounded sheep, beyond
these post-harvest fields of ash, beyond
these silent silos, these testimonials
to our hunger.

The Shearing Shed

We come off the runway
& into the Shearing Sheds Motel
in a pre-twilight haze.

We find a room facing west,
unshaded,
though I have no desire to stare
into the shitty glare of a Dubbo sunset.

I can't get a drink at the bar.
There's a CLOSED sign
on the only door
& the fridge is empty.

We call Reception
for some milk & a razor
but there's no answer.

Hungry after the 750 kilometer stretch
from Broken Hill, the kids are calling for a meal.
We feed on McDonalds — imported beef
from across the street, then settle for bed.

I lie down with my eyes open
& stare at shadows of shearing sheds.

There's this corrugated shed
which looks like an aircraft hangar
& from a certain angle
this reminds Allison of the barracks
she & her parents lived in
when they first arrived in Australia
back in '65: "What did it feel like
to be packed in like sheep?" I ask.

There's no answer.

Allison has fallen asleep & the kids
are travelling in their dreams —
their small bodies twitching
in their beds, & Lachlan
cuts his cheek
on the edge of something sharp:
a close shave with the idea of flight.

The Old HQ Holden

I remember red sand
on his windscreen,
how it obscured things:
that road out in front, those white lines
approaching, repeating, appearing
then disappearing, like bad jokes,
until he ran out of gas.

At the side of the road
behind the visitors' map to Mungarani
I scooped red soil
as thick as the palm of my hand
& looked towards the horizon
at the distance I would have to walk
beneath the brim of my hat.

When I tried to crank him back up
he barked with dry throat —
a bird, high up, circled
recorded our presence
like a ring on a map
marks a waterhole.

I stood beside him for shade
waiting for someone
to put us back on track
but nobody came.

Then he watched me leave
on foot
a stick figure with his thumb out
knowing I'd return to him
with my jerry-can
like an arsonist, red dirt
& fire in my eyes,
to take him home.

***

I left footprints where I had walked
behind me
but found wooden stumps & wire
with my fingertips
& a wind
not unlike a voice
carried my prints away
as if they were salt
& temporary.

Below a scaling sun
my lizard skin peeled back
the surface of a stone
& I saw bones
through the salt-drenched ribs
of leafless things.

I returned to him
paler than dead wood
with my jerry-can full.

***

I took him home
spoke about our history
our dry voyage
of things left behind —
spare wheels, blown tyres
& oil patches on the side of the road

We had cruised the sunset country
in search of relics, artefacts
for leftover bits of old things:
useable parts, moveable scraps
things thrown out, or simply
discarded.

We brought our findings home
& piled them up on top of each other
like bodies in a cemetery —
then prayed over them
until someone came
& took them away
until we had nothing but ourselves
& our half-forgotten stories
to live with.

***

And now he's that broken down car
parked out front, rubber-less & rusted
from all those mission trips, nothing but
a stripped shell
with a speck of red sand in his ear
like an echo inside
a beached shell, a poem, a derelict house
waiting for a fire
to burn out; I can tell
by the flame in his eye
that small things have stayed too long
like kidney stones, & pain,
memories which won't go away.

***

You looked in the papers
& found that car FOR SALE
but the price tag was too high
& you said, "There's too much work to be done on it."
So, I did what had to be done.

I dragged that old car down into the back paddock
where he couldn't be seen from the road.
There, in tall grass, I poured petrol on his
peeling skin & with a match, set him alight.

I watched him burn the late afternoon
like a premature sunset, until the sky above
resembled a charred thing, black ash raining
from the apocalyptic negative of a heavenly cloud.

When narcissistic night spread
its long-legged shroud of darkness
I took my bone warmed body
home to an uncomfortable bed

where I dreamt of open roads, deserts,
the broken things between us, how much
I needed him, apologising, for not letting go
when he'd had enough

& when I woke, the following morning, I saw him
distant but present, gazing up at those hills
as if he were alive, as if he'd never left,
as if he weren't mine, in the first place.

St. Kilda Mangrove Trail, early morning

A seed drops slowly. Leaf
by yellow leaf. Ripe berry
bushes, lavender, pink
sea-heath & stunted
samphire voyage across
wooden walkways.

Below prayer-red knees
colonial Christmas spiders
wave puzzled silk saltbush
petitions, which I vaguely
grasp at with guide books

& History lessons
that recall the pick
& barrow beginnings of a city
tackling the Great Depression
in Keynesian labour schemes

& how it set its sights beyond suburbs,
stonewalling
a sweeping swamp's debate
& sub-dividing
saltfield into pastures

that would never be sown
by human hands.

Open-ended mangroves rise
beneath an unemployably pale blue sky,
wait for high tide, correspondence
from a conference of crabs, reportage
from mouth-spill of royal spoonbill
& shearwater journalists, their hunger
dissolving iron in fluid air.

Silver-smooth wings coat
the aquatic surface of our industrious eyes.

Hard to believe
we're only just beginning to hear
the humanity beneath their flight,
the currents of possibility
which allow us to ask
whether Nature has ever been stalled,
or these trickling nunga tears,
dawn's low tide creeks
running backwards, as light
through Time, recording
the passage of a fragile promise:
to return when we are gone.

Dry Creek Trail

1.

We jump a white gate
& descend on crushed quartz
through History, along a trail
between conifer & creek
behind Yatala jail.

2.

We find pages flung
from cell block windows
over a penal landscape:
outstations, fences, quarries
& sheds (that once sucked water
from fluent creek to flooded cell)
follow a design in clay
& shale beside huts & cubicles
& a flying fox on a pedestal, a cable
suspended between parent & child,
& a fortress, its walls tipped
with broken glass, unable
to shelter the stone
& iron box
from our eyes

though it contains nothing,
no lighting nor ventilation
but a single candle on the floor
that has burnt down to its core.

3.
Outside, we spy
a steady stream of cynical hikers:
a man with Hotel Alcatraz
on his T-shirt, perhaps
a tourist, & families
collecting History,
smooth pebbled visions
on sandbar asylums, leashed dogs
dragging their wardens toward
the shadows of piss-scented trees,
youths in prohibited areas, bicyclists
& joggers, lovers on stepping stones
beneath the causeway
as children run Indian file
along its stonegrass banks
or lift themselves
onto lookout railings
perhaps searching for things
we have not yet seen.

Morialta Falls

Our sun-skinned children climb
stone-cut stairs to a cave, a caped belfry
from which their wild crazy calls
bite at the apple of distance
and stretch the boundaries of tenderness

while beneath their bracken dry feet
the half-broken shell of a bush hen's egg
resonates with the crackled rasp of their laughter.

They kick small colonies of stone into space,
watch them fall to where the convict masonry
the heavy amulets and charms of the past
have been laid across the sandy riverbed.
With accuracy each sunburnt rock will tread
water, its secret search for relief as intrepid
as forty thousand years, channelled in exile.

These sentient sun-bats know the way
back to us as surely as sonar, schoolish
wings transparent, talons which grip
each chipped and scaled face
with the stoney precision of skeletal

scrub, every nerve fibre carved
with eucalyptic constellations, dark
meanings, the transference restless
beneath sleeping sand, something
we dig into with parrot eyes from
dry bush steeples, only to find
the shallow graves of fallen things,
an exposure in the absence of water,
a suddenness that offers no release
though winter flowers bloom
upon the faces of our children.

Lizard Rock Walking Trail

for the children of Folland Park Kindergarten

We emerge where straight golden lines of sun emerge
on worn dirt walking trail, struggle as briefly as History
through the weed of a turnstile, and our hushed voices
sweep aside the curative melaleuca, search for things
we do not have words for: there's something urban
behind us, as unforgettable as a call for *bili bili ata* —
our ground strokes have become as white as footsteps
on the slow blown ashes of unspoken Time. We listen

to Maa's open-ended story, to the pantomimic code beside
humpy made of fallen sticks. A tongue beats into daylight.
Our red-eyed guide stop-starts upon every black boy
and creek bed, upon every outcrop of whittled granite, and
upon our sunburnt cheeks the windless flora. He points,
"Can y'see him?" and we all turn glaze-faced towards
the crazed far ridge, snaking clay-red trails and a blue
hand tearing a hole in a sky unmade for our eyes.

we seem to be looking everywhere we're not

Yet the echo, twin & shadow, play of pure sound on ear captures

distance, & those straight golden lines wave back,

share space with the absurdly sun-split word, "coo-ee" —

the torn shifting vowel, a splinter of conscience between

silences, searches for what cannot be seen, waits

for our own voices to return, until the feral shape

of Lizard Rock looms beneath the signifying gestures

of his land: here, it's as if our small voices have awoken

something larger than sound — an enormous grey head

on the verge, rock-warm neck carved in light,

blue tongue withheld for greater discourses,

while his eyes, his defiant eyes, bask

unforbidden in those straight golden lines of sun.

Ground Water

Summer approaches with a promise of thirst,
a presence of mind bottled at the hip,
the blue-capped range rising in the West
like an alternate Mecca, to be ascended
or stripped of reason.

At the end of the Upper Colo Road
a lyre bird scuttles with its twin until beneath
a cross-thatch of poorly cut lantana, they disappear.

The outbreak of fencelines that has followed us
seems to have found a cure, some private act
of diminishment as the final gate falls away
& lets us through. In this tie-dyed wilderness
air mists with the illicit scent of oil burners,
candles & incense. Naked charms flop in feral cleavages
without demand. There is touch
& unrestrained movement as we are led into Eden, the
unchallenged river an unscorched sound stroking the
swollen earth beside us.

In every smile there is a letting go, an idea found

in each spoken word, the utterance of nourishment

that rises up like ground water

from somewhere deep inside, or below,

the torn canvas of things that have been driven

underground, & allowed to turn:

a certain moistness

that we now press softly

to our parched & searching lips.

Searching for Mawson

Hobart, April 2001

From the red deck of the *aurora australis,* his blue-tipped
lips press their coldness to my pale skin, thoughts frozen
like an ice scene outside
the memorabilia of an Antarctic hut: nude limbs,
& sauna-white mind, rushing outdoors screaming towards
another level of awakening before the frost-bitten
numbness of his fingers returned to haunt every trace of
remembrance, a land where flesh
once tingled with the sun's applause.

And at that moment of consummation,
as if Time itself had come, or ended, the act
that once stood suspended washed
the stone of some distant, frozen impediment
into the keeled pools of our darkest thoughts
& needs, where we sensed the folly of his hope:
his smooth tongue lost to a sunless Winter,
untreated timbers that stiffened & cracked beneath
the impact of his waiting, a neck stretched around
the throat of his dreams.

These untoured eyes, careless in their comfort zones
watch, & are seen, with the same
uneasy gestures pleading for deliverance,
for some ancient shuttle of desire
to cut & thrust its barbaric way back home
to thrash across an open sea until
bruised & wind-blasted it might come to rest

in this unlisted harbour; & here, it would lie between the
hot thighs of a lover's cultural landscape
recalling the roll & reel of rescue, the essence
of salvation in the energetic shape of a ship
that lost its way, but understood with a certain grace
the nature of the ground it searched for,
& the water over which it had to travel to find us.

Country Of Innocence

Sacred
snow-capped mountain
melts,
ushers the learning thaw
toward oceans.

swift rivers running quietly out of breath

They gather shells
like exchange students
on their first beach
            & off shore
collect coral & bone.

fragile eco-symptoms of impermanence

I dream they are diving
on the wreck of a ship
that has no final destination
but I am mistaken.

They return home
like trout
fighting their way upstream —
the snow in their eyes.

S/now Country

There's a slow avalanche of images
melting in my memory.

Out of winter storage
snow-ridden ranges
thaw into rivers.

Clear ideas — holiday, I think, 1980.

Feathery trout leap towards
the charity of artificial flies.

Families of fishers
flaunt the longest rods
in the shallowest water
where rocks as crisp
as shivering light at sunrise
reveal a river's two white banks
embracing the splintered trunk
of a fallen river gum.

Winter has bandaged
the broken angler
for posterity.

Balancing on
soft snow edges,
children reel in fish,
toy with thoughts,
imagine taking the cast off
this alabaster world,
floating skin kites
on a wind of change.

The abseiling sky
lets down a rope
for children to climb
into its clouded eyes
before sunset
turns their world to blood.

A lone climber
listens to the unstoppable
sounds of a country
in transition, remembers
the bleeding surface of an Antarctic ice-shelf:
the crack, the fissure, the thunderous
breaking away of silence.

Remembers floating beneath
the lights of the Southern Cross.

Adds to his list a snow-field
melting into Spring —
something else worth
to remember
another value added
to the melting currency of sound.

I walk, a snapple of frost
beneath my feet.
I wake, leaf-damp impressions
where I have stepped.

Snow slides off all surfaces
& every silky aureole begs
to be pinched.

Overhead, dross-laden branches
milk matrimonial veils,
sacred spider-webs,
clothes-lines of deceit

daring the slightest touch
— wingtip, breeze, a shake —
to interrupt
the span of this suspended silence.

Banality & The Archaeologist

Working with bare hands on
permafrost dripping knees I
dig for old bones & cast them in
Plaster-of-Paris names for posterity —
a resurrected range of Latin offers
dignity even for those difficult-to-name
& hard-to-get-at banalities though
I can't quite make out what I'd call
a new species like Java Man or the
Qantassaurus if I had the opportunity:
would I name my new found banality
after a sponsor or a country, perhaps
something more appropriate, or colder?
My casts don't pretend to heal. I curse
the almost impenetrable layers of earth
as if they were horizontal tombstones
to house the dead, then listen to a dry-
marrow-crunch as the newly named fall
apart in my ice-hardened hands. My
skin-blistered exertion holds back
someone else's impatience. Above the
stacking sound of stepped-upon-bones
a sang-froidian song from a saraband

of the sky turns into an icy wind-pocket
& chills the dig with silence.

In the thawing academic mirror something
as immediate & brittle as a word snaps
a collector's ice-T lips into a smile &
his teeth crack away from dead nerves
as ice from the Arctic shelf of a frozen skull.

Mine, I think, & squeeze the last drop
of toothless sun from my eyes. Tomorrow,
I'll remember to bring the gloves.

The Herring-boats

for my mother

"...out from the reef the call of the seals
sounded like the cries of the shipwrecked..."

August Strindberg

With faces rain-wet
the herring-boats go out
past long dead piers & breakers,
their fore sails ruffled — yellowish
as commodore epaulettes
crumbling on Ulysses' naked shoulders —
carrying a cargo of flak jackets
to fight against a tidal chill
which sweeps over every deck-bound body.
To the bridge
as waves push passed
like customs officers in a hurry.
Sailors suck wind, their bellies empty,
& squeeze their limbs beneath wire,
hook-lines & ropes — all hands
to pulley, block & tackle —
then scrolled white spinnaker
unscrolls, & a great light

fills the canopy, her bow lifts into clouds
& an open sea advances
like the green asphodel fields of Elysium.

***

Circe tacks towards an unconquered sea,
sirens shrieking from shore,
the night's table laid fresh
beyond wooden doors,
signs of things that come & go,
left behind.

She looks down,
deep into green waters
& sees yellow alabaster vases
as still as rigor mortis
in their broken packing cases.

"She begged for water to relieve her nausea."

Circe casts her suspicious nets
across entanglements,
stitches between reefs
filled with fleeting,
momentary pauses of fear.

Her knock-knees & arms
cross over like sand bars
in shallow pools of submerged thought
& scrape the sunken hulls of misadventure.

Fishing for fate
Circe suspects cowardice
but suspicion,
weakened by labour,
has become a statue on shore
staring out through curtains
that are never quite closed.

Her eyes have become waves
that wash over the painted eyes
on the bows of the herring-boats.

A Greek tragedy,
her eyes follow a similar path
searching for answers
in the split wake of those boats
that never return.

***

In the crow's nest
writing fake IOUs,
the sacred lines
on navigation charts never used,
Ulysses watches
the upturned legs of masts
in centre squall.

Memories float home to Penelope
like fire extinguishers at sunset
to reconcile
with ancient instrumentation of beating heart,
the flesh of fantasy & paranoia.

Investigator of human desire,
Ulysses lets go
only to be reminded
of what he has lost,
what he no longer holds in his arms
but places his trust in.

Then, far from shore
the jealous steeples rise
like a chain of faithless mountains.

The salty semen of an ocean
ejaculates

& the herring-boats go down,
all hands sensing

with new sea-weed organs
a subtle stretching of surf.

Trapped
in voice-pockets of diminishing sound
their ideas struggle for air.

The capsized drown in secret symphony,
sore throats stuffed with shore-sand.

***

When Circe reaches
these human hulls,
she dives after
what she cannot possess,
& discovers
a swirl of conch shells
which she lifts to her lips,
listens
to the sound of suburban hunting horns
that echo
from the vast discourse
of her own defiance.

Found

These hulls are superstructures floating
in cigar-box paradise. You take your Cuban

neat — no ice. And don't ask what an island
is doing here, amidst all this driftwood luxury.

Playing at hotels, I guess. The maritime boat
-shaped souvenir shop in trance. Or transit.

Taste testing vintage sand in this little bay
of literary pigs. There's something Havana-like

"in the way" you quickly run over your theme
& reverse, reverse your theme & run over it

again, to ensure everything's at least one day's
drive away from your reader. Capable of being seen

from a distance, tiny characters swimming in citrus
-free water where speed-boats ride on Jeff Buckley

waves. The body yet to be found, or dragged from sea-
weed floor; further out than in, you land again

on beachside deck. Here, you could be anyone sipping
Singha beer or gin slings, watching a sperm whale

making love to a wave, not knowing its tail from its arse.
Direction is an after-dinner drinks thought just off-shore

listening to ol' Blue Eyes announcing with his over
-wracked throat to all and sundry "I Did It My Way"

on that dial-a-voice telephone, the plastic isthmus
grasped firmly between the twin lands of speak & listen.

Just a child who everyone wants to adopt. After all, *this*
could be Istanbul: near enough, but not close enough, to

Mt. Ararat. Just an aerial shot of an ark. Ribs of things found in
absurdia, a collection of half-hearted dreams &

disturbed world views from which you wake to find yourself
searching for proof, though the evidence

is just not there.

My Country, Sometimes

Give me this Champion Ruby
roll-your-own country, this dream-
rock rubbed with paperthin signs,
its gum still wet & dripping passed
the necessary hour of my & yours.

Hand the Government Health Warning
around with may & might; perhaps, forget
about those dodgy didge interruptions —
in my country, sometimes Undara
is bent out of cultural shape
in the weed collector's hands.

Another hollow pipe sharing
Murray's shot-gun experiences.
You breathe in, & out, & time
is suspended long enough
to ask, Is this Amphora,
a product or slogan
in propaganda heaven?

Warzone incense burns bridges
& the candle of deadly dawn
welcomes Undara by the Hudson —
flowing, slowly flowing, watering down

fragile promises, & thirst
is a throat in the grip of Pacific rim fingers.

Dry lips leave an imprint
as smoke rings lose their way back
to earth.

Here, all reason is classical mud
sinking in a mangrove of Maloufian
alliteration
while mild
miscellaneous thoughts
drift into malleable air —
squelching, softly squelching
wetlands of weekend guitar thumb
& strum interpretations of things
untranslatable; unrhymable ifs & buts
burning protestors' roach-ended fingertips
until there is no standing room available.

I listen to the politician
on my answering machine:
though the microphone
falls from his magnificent mouth,
the people at the rear of the room
have already left for another smoke,
& a chance to catch up on tomorrow.

The Pipeline

In passing on what it has found
the mining company marks its position
on the miracle map of "this is yours
& this is mine" with a surprise attack,
an asterisk, a pirate's cross carved
into the exact location of a natural resource,
as if it were an idea: how a contour sensitive
pipeline might stay in character, carry
water between those who find
& those who pay.

"for what they are about to receive"

Yet, something primal
in this method of sharing —
the way one divines utopia
as a rite of corporate passage:
the ceremonial cleansing of hands
with dusty leaves before
the customary committee hand-dance,
the typical exchange of sympathy
& detail shaken by an act of subversion,
an agreement roughly "coming-to-terms"

with a papery-thin human presence
wrapped around a stone heart
in a star-shaped desert; things
this country's closed fist cannot hide
from the global glint in its government's
drier than dry eyes.

Beach Broken
for Glen

I'm a swimming speck of saline flesh in a wave's
glare, paddling out beyond a last blur of playground
breakers, my body morphed into pale liquid like eyes
under glass, half-submerged in a swollen murmur
of water that is passing through & around all I will
ever be. & I watch a hushless gullet of spuming
bleach-throated anger as it scream-stretches gurgling
tonsil trails of tidal fluid towards the ambivalent
undertow of point break — a place where two rolling
white arms clench-link their gnarled hands & curl
-crush the nothingness between — but down breaking
sediments, worldly impediments whirling in the bore's
ten-fold return to whale-less shore, & up breaking
like snow-shells on clear-cut images of sand. This fibro
board snaps at an on-coming braille of waves, catches
the first crest, then peaks out to a sudden loss of gravity,
collapses as the sea-bed sucks in a breath, & I'm waxed
'n ready to break in this last clutch at stability as an ocean
spills its salty opus & scoops up my soul & I'm breaking
out, surfing the vortex of this hydro-dynamic library, my
words splashing & switching through swash-buckling
schisms of gushing Aquarius, & breaking from these
twisting tubes of childhood, I break through.

Ghost Riders

After the fire in Judith Wright's *bora ring*
I could see that homeless rider struggling
in blackness
to say what could not be said
— to name what had been done —
heart heavy with the ashen shadows of fallen things
a word forming & unforming
around the perimeter of bush circles
that were designed to describe
the grief
but the unsaid word is no longer in shadow —
what was bloody murder then,
is bloody murder now:

I hear it sung over the four corners of gravesites
where there are no bars from which a body might hang in
final repose, to suffer in silence — their bodies kneel in
sacred margins praying
to a parrot god, politicians & clergy singing
empty songs of lounge-room sorrow
in cinemas of common despair.

I hear it trembled on lips rimming
the last broken circle
where tourists photograph dancers
in cultural display.

I hear it in souvenir shops where painted bodies
are anatomised on postcards & bric-a-brac.

I hear it whispered in hospital corridors far from
playgrounds littered with kerosene cans & used plastic
bags that cling like glue to ghost rides, far
from creek beds scattered with beer torn cartons
& broken bottles in back alleys where needles jab
in hepatitis dark, cradled in the arms of social workers.

Jarinyanu Story Cycle: Kurtal Leaves Adelaide

Jarinyanu David Downs
Great Sandy Desert 1925 — Adelaide 1995

Pale Kurtal sits thin-lipped beside me, his squatting body
balancing heart-driven veins with upraised arms,
generating
grey clouds as I write, his thunderous storm rides north
& I remember watching him go, his swollen ghost heels
rising beyond my green grasp — this is Jarinyanu, this is
Kurtal as rainmaker, as street shifting cloud, as soft
shadow
kicking on ahead, towards his own country.

There's a flash flood down my driveway, water swirls
around a steel lamp post, suburban light house, leaves
memories behind, images of things uprooted,
& I'm reaching
for his feet, his transparent ankles large enough
to appear
close when he lifts off, levitates as if cloud tripping
& I watch his five-fingered fists gripping the great white
accordian

of lateral thought, a cloud grid metamorphosing

into cell bars,

or the threat of heaven as another prison

but held

above his head like a weight, or the bright bulb

of a question:

how long before it will fall, before he will come

back to earth

& reveal his map magic, stories of human

rivers

flowing between waterholes, mangroves north

& south.

Into the distance Kurtal carries blue rain lines, iconic

bucket

for catching symbolic clouds, a cyclone of ideas waiting

for sunrays to seep around their splitting edges, bringing

their damp smell of familiality, that sense of things

which return

to haunt us, but Kurtal is drifting away, taking the

abundance

of Winter with him, & I am alone, only the thunder fading

into the north to remind me, of the things he leaves

behind,

the places I've yet to visit, if only in the mind.

The Handover
The Strehlow Collection, 1999

In "The Gallery" above Megaw & Hogg three hundred
& sixty one lots plus a cheap catalogue detailing
expectations & disappointments flake like bone wrapped

in white tissue paper memories turning to dust beneath
glass the gaze returned as a simple reflection in the son's
eyes a diary discarded along with family history &

photographs of a dead white father with black friends
lined along a wall behind a partition The Management
state are not to be seen by uninitiated men or women or

children but we've seen this all before in glossy German
magazines the wisdom of naked flesh & the intimate embrace of
men devoted to the metamorphosis of things

worth passing on or handing down from father to son
the sacred object of self on public wall before the fall
from grace & the auctioneer's unpolished hammer.

Canvas As Crime Scene

I feel like a criminal
even though I haven't done anything
but moisten a face, or two,
painting over those things I've found
in need of a coat of paint.

Perhaps it is a crime to doodle,
to draw
(as if from a well of emotion)
in the margins of someone else's painting?

Sometimes I wonder what belongs to me.
What can I say belongs to me?
If all history
is the history of ownership,
the story of a longing
to belong to something
that cannot be held in
my hands, begins
with someone else.

The history I paint in blood
is fluid is relating,

without order,

without personal space,

without common structure.

When placed on someone's canvas,

I am someone else's history,

a lover with a vision

one can no longer identify with,

an impression of emptiness

for anyone to complete,

a self who has no history.

I watch while you brush with death,

stepping in my salt-water puddles,

mangroves & tear-ducts, places where

I have left too much space

for you to follow.

Left alone for too long

the paint begins to dry & crack.

& I have nothing better to do

with my spare time.

Pokok Kayu

Is this filling of spare time
just a way of learning ancient crafts,
borrowing tongues that can't be brought back
as easily as these ideas
speaking out of tongue.

Perhaps this is the irony of courtship: almost
the language of another
taking root
in a lover's empty dowry,
the gift grafted to these gossip-thin
stems of life, these
status swollen lines
as simple as ancestry
or treachery.

Gestures come from all angles,
slide off all arbitrary surfaces.

The unknown shape of wind
suddenly given meaning
changes everything
as a curtain blows over a window sill

& drags upon the stationary frame
as complacently
as a married couple's question
or cry for recognition.

The way that fabric moves
ever so slowly between the inside
& the outside
shapes the frame of this room.

Within this shape
an old photograph clings
to a piece of cardboard —

a snapshot worn
around the edges
like an old sarong.

the soft sense of something captured

A dancer empowered,
the stance of a warrior
reduced to an image,
like a tree trapped

on a gust of social change,

forever captive in calligraphic pose
amber dripping from her wounds.

Those captivating leaves
leaning towards tomorrow;
another unadorned autumn.

Her sap heavy costume
as dark as dried blood,
holds her up
like a wind-break, a tree
that has learnt how to stand
on its own, though
a face looks out at us
through the thin bark of its mortality.

When the wind blows
a warm warning
she bends
but does not break.

Her head cocked with cosmology
takes everything in,
absorbs all light

until she becomes a shape,
an echo, or shadow,

brought into the world
through another's womb.

We face each other
like shades
animating the living,
our two bodies alligned
with mutual ancestry.

My dreams fall as leaves to her feet,
imitate the skeletons of lost words,
forgotten pains, recent memories
that scatter before a second wind.

My leaves float as musical notes,
levitate & drift into their own arrangements
around the melody of her body,
the composition of her skin
stretched with meaning.

New shoots sprout
from the living surface of a forgotten tune.

I see her arms
inching towards mine
but we do not touch.

Her feet embrace the earth
as if they were divining rods
announcing a water birth.

A fresh spring beneath
the fading foundations of our world.

When the north wind lifts her eyes
tears pool at her feet,
a fresh rain on my face.

Virtual Cemeteries

I saw a film about the Mandelbrot set
enormous fractals in living space
spreading colourfully from limb to fig
& a science fiction writer unfolding
cyberspace with visions of a mobile village
spoke with the silence of intellect.

Fossilised bones & dinosaur impressions
are cut from living rock & no one
stands in the way of commercial progress
as the Bradshaw Collection goes under
the hammer of collective bargaining
in ancient rite of community.

Somewhere between earth & space
the veins are cutting blood lines
from the flesh of Reason, needles
squirt prevention as plastic over
-rides the exchange of body fluids:
you will live & die, & your coffin will

be made from the skin of open scars
& we will have access to your gravesite
via the internet, the headstones
will read like credits, & we will visit
the tomb of Lenin, the crypt of Mao,
the plot of Marx, & grief will be an option.

Peter, Carl Jung, & Me

1.

Metaphysics

Peter says things, words
                  like "mysticism"
& "universal" —
            a rock in my hand
but who can judge its weight?
           When I throw it high
it does not cling to the sun
           it stares momentarily
grasps at the possibility of itself
           then falls back to earth.

2.

Don Giovanni's

We could talk for hours
                      & never repeat ourselves —
"These are my dreams," says Peter
                      "though I do not pretend
to understand them."

Through the one-way meniscus of the restaurant
I imagine Carl's stained-glass window
                the lion & the naked woman
                a crucifix & the battle for superiority
the way he is portrayed beneath
                      as someone we might look up to.

This is Don Giovanni's; a waiter
                      hovers near our table.

3.

Manners

Peter consumes

cannelloni shaped like a giant cowrie shell

something vastly different waiting

to be convinced of its difference

starting from the inside

as if he were gutting a boneless fish

& emptying an offal of original words

into the vast unknown of my disbelief.

Digestion

is just a summary

of what we haven't said.

4.

Kangaroo Island

I dream I am an island
    but there is no water
only the sound of waves lapping
    against an invisible shoreline.

I drag my tongue over rocks
    breaking away from a continent
swallow the crust
    then drink red wine to wash it down.

I think of an armpit, the smell
    of dry sweat, my head curled
awkwardly into some unnameable position
    as I try to sleep on your words.

Media/Slick

Did anyone notice the oil slick

on the front page   — French coast

with toast —   crumbs & vegemite stains

on this morning's table cloth

(as if difference

were a matter of size,   a quantity

not a location)

— a thumbprint

vernacular, nicotined fingers rubbing

as unconscious as erasure over

the fine print

— a stain spreading

Russian caviar into rock pools &

petroleum pregnant roe as big as wet

footballs rolled up like turf & dropped

into buckets, ten gallon drums shipped

back to the bad taste refinery (for processing?)

haste wants waste: "wisdom is the folly of age"

In a tacked-on weekend magazine
someone is advertising novelty coats
for crude-coated angry penguins.

Horses, cats, dogs parading eco-friendly fashions
in a muddled Murdochian catalogue.

Red wine spills — a Beaujolais — & a yellow dish
-cloth arrives to mop up the mess.

                  I sprinkle salt

before the residue
(of a Century's hard drinking)
leaves an impression on my New Year's carpet.

Beachwalk

I draw the morning landscape
around me like a towel
spread on sand

& my daughter
follows me
like a little xerox

her tiny footprints
copying mine
in miniature

shells
scalloped by toes
that hardly make a dent

in wet sand
chasing seagulls
for crumbs

she stops
as if stung
& watches

birds painting
their exile
on blue sky

& with red eyes
wrapped around
her sunburnt shoulders

I follow
her back
the way we came.

Refugees

There is nowhere to hide.

They find me
& come ashore, walk
the long white mile of my beach
their clothes stitched in sand
& at the crest of every dune
they cast their eyes about
searching for some clue
as to my indifference.

How can I tell them
that there is nothing
more to me than this,
that the oasis is a mirage
& the sky an echo
of every sound
they've heard before.

Remains

The bones are so scorched
& sand-brittle
it's possible to think
these lovers had wings
which burst into flame
as they tried to touch the sun.

The further I hike
across this naked basin
of tangled bone
the greater the sound
of a migratory silence
in every broken shell
I raise to my ear.

These lovers are lost to our grasp.

Their alien, annexed syllables
speak from beyond the quartz
& amber of history, float
in richer sands than these small
minute grains which fall
from my unloving hands.

On The Rough Edge

On the rough edge of Lake Eyre
I squeeze salt back into defiant water,
a body immersed in a fist of cosmic blue.

Aphrodite shimmies beside coded clouds.
Messages are sent between: invisible
a twisted indigo upon my neck.

Down on knees only a dim awareness
of her impermanence; how she ascends
from Hades on a wind of dedicated charts

& courses, her movement from night
into the mercurial banner of morning,
the position of a star, her rise

& repose — head resting in my hands;
at the crossroads, a mirror buried
with two pebbles, black & white

& the fall of a feather conjures a meeting,
a consummation, the liberation of Hermes
from the grasp of her salty tongue.

Sometimes The Beach Gets Depressed

I gather in this dark place
without name, or speech
moonshadow on sand
beneath my bare feet
immovable, as a barrage
of thought, & night
as black as skin, a brother
with his hand out, asking
for more than I can give.

Night as black as falling
into this.

Nothing moves this country.
Its shape a great nothingness
preparing for something less
to raise a single hair on my body.

Beyond my reach
the sand dunes are waves
held in dark suspension
by an unclothed stillness.

Even the water
is naked, caught
without its wind.

Stripped of pretension
a new sea mounts
the seductive horizon.

his melancholy afterglow

I wait
as hot as foreskin
for a grain of sand
to pull me back from
the brink of an inevitable
king tide — a desire
so overwhelming
it could drown me
for another two hundred years.

NOTES

My Country, Sometimes: Undara is in North
Queensland. Undara Dawn is a piece of mood music
composed by didgeridoo player, David Hudson. The
intentional though inoffensive play on the
composer's name refers to the Hudson River, USA,
in a way which suggests an American influence upon
indigenous music.

Jabiluka Honey: refers to the Jabiluka uranium mine
in the Kakadu Heritage Reserve — Senator Hill
sought permission from the United Nations for a
mine to operate in the area, and was given it, but the
Gundjehmi people have refused permission for Rio
Tinto to mine the site. Extensive establishment
operations have polluted the waterways and clear-
felling has devastated the once pristine area.

St. Kilda Mangrove Trail: refers to the 100 Acres of
Adelaide which were sub-divided into pastoral land,
and developed by the unemployed during the Great
Depression through Liberal government funded
work schemes — the poem was written when John
Howard introduced Work For The Dole to the false
announcement that work for the dole had its origins
in Labour government policy.

The Pipeline: refers to the artesian basin recently found in a remote region of eastern Western Australia.

Pokok Kayu: is Bahasa Indonesia for a stump of an apparently dead tree from which new branches suddenly sprout. Dawan, who the photograph refers to, was the first female warrior in Balinese dance — prior to the 1950s women were not allowed to be portrayed as warriors — she assumes the *baris* (power stance) in the photograph. An earlier version of this poem appears in Kalimat: An Arabic-Australian Literary Quarterly.

Lizard Rock Walking Trail — Gadno Rock (Lizard Rock) Walking Trail, Para Wirra Recreation Park, Kuarna country, 8.11.2001: *bili bili ata* — request for silence when hunting; *humpy* — shelter; *Maa* — character from Kuarna dreamtime, a galah who knew how to make fire. Kuarna is pronounced 'Ga-na'.

ACKNOWLEDGEMENTS

Poems in this collection have been published in *AnotherSun* (UK), *Calende* (Romania), *Coppertales*, *Core, Famous Reporter, Flow: Friendly Street Reader 25, Friendly Street Reader 26, Hobo, Homebrew, Idiom 23 , Imago, Island, JAAM* (NZ)*, Kalimat, New England Review, Overland, Prospect Review, Retort, SideWaLK, Social Alternatives, Southern Ocean Review* (NZ)*, Subverse QPF Anthology, Republic Reader, Takahe* (NZ)*, The Adelaide Review, The Ardent Sun, The Colonial Athens, The Gawler Bunyip, The Weekend Australian, Thylazine,* & *Vernacular.*

I wish to express my sincere gratitude to the Australia Council and ARTSA, and all the people who have offered encouragement and support for this collection of poetry, especially Professor Thomas Shapcott AO, and Dr. John von Sturmer. Also Jan Owen, Peter Eason, Shelton Lea, Mike Ladd, Heather Sladdin, Glen Murdoch, John West, Karen Knight, Les Wicks, Paul Hardacre, Duncan Kentish, Rob Scott and Jeff Dale, and the numerous editors of literary publications who've published my writing over the years.

I'd also like to thank my family, for being there through thick and thin.